AF572025

Toward Desire

Linda Lee Harper

Winner of the 1995 Word Works Washington Prize

The Word Works • Washington, DC

First Edition, First Printing
Toward Desire

Printed in the U.S.A.
Book design, typography by Joyce Mulcahy, Jude Langsam
Cover art by Barbara Kerne, "Homage to the Earth Spirits," a woodcut print on artist-made paper

Library of Congress Number: 95-062219
International Standard Book Number: 0-915380-33-1

The following poems, some in slightly different versions, appeared in: "Effie Swears," "At the Other Grandfather's Door"–*The Georgia Review;* "Ben 1"–*The Connecticut River Review;* "Before the Knife"–*The Charlotte Poetry Review;* "Sissy"–*The Bridge;* "Crossing the Border"–*The Laurel Review;* "Teaching Composition"–*The Massachusetts Review;* "May"–*Phase & Cycle;* "For a Flower Girl Posing," "Hitting the Deck"–*Ohio Poetry Review;* "Lucy"–*The Antigonish Review;* "First Ride"–*West Branch;* "Elsie's Lament"–*Horizons,* S.C. Writer's Anthology; "Little Sisters of the Poor"–*Horizons,* Best of Issue; "Apologies to Ethel Mae"–*Blue Unicorn;* "Fishing Alone," "Duet"–*International Quarterly;* "Favoring Andy," "In Pennsylvania Spring"–*Kansas Quarterly;* "Almost Born Again"–*South Coast Poetry Journal;* "Swimming Past God"–*The Piedmont Literary Review;* "Vanities"–*The Hawai'i Review;* "The Curse"–*The Illinois Review;* "Their Fathers Were Beautiful," "Hollis"–*Great River Review.*

Some of the poems appear in my chapbook, *A Failure of Loveliness*, the William and Kingman Page Award winner (Nightshade Press, 1994). "Effie Swears," "Vanities," "Favoring Andy," and "Son Remembers," also appear in *45/96, The Ninety-Six Sampler of South Carolina Poetry* (Furman University: Ninety-Six Press, 1994). "Her Mother's Lament" and "Little Sisters of the Poor" appear in the SCWW anthology *Horizons*, 1994. "Little Sisters" was selected as Best of Issue.

I want to thank the Corporation of Yaddo and the Virginia Center for the Creative Arts for residencies during which I completed or began many of the poems included here. Thanks also to Bud Kohr, Mildred Brandeberry, Hilda, and Ethel Mae, Kate and Ben, to Phebe Davidson for her friendship and to Paul for his relentless patience. Special thanks to Hilary Tham for her sensitive editing and lyrical encouragement.

For Paul

The body moves, though slowly, toward desire.
We come to something without knowing why.

"The Manifestation," T. Roethke

Table of Contents

3 *Swimming Past God*

4 *The Accident*

◆ Crossing the Border

This one isn't the one where the river
cuts the land like a dying stream of piss.
It's not the one where snow bleaches
horizons into hard-scrubbed curbs cold
enough for a witch's tit to freeze shut.

It's the one at the end of the day.
The one, last word before you storm out the door.
The good, hard kick the dog endures
when the alimony checks stop coming in
or start going out.
The scratch you key into the blue Jaguar
parked too close to your Ford.
It's been known to lie somewhere between
your best friend's wife's knees
and ample opportunity.
Or his daughter's.

If you look carefully,
you can see the tail of those
who trekked out before you.
The messages they send back,
like ships in a bottle,
tell you nothing is impossible
to offend if you whittle time down
to exquisite trivialities,
each essential outrage
as delicately rendered as a scrimshaw comb
you wear in your hair or pocket
like a charm to ward off good luck,
to fend off reasonable compromise,
or precipitous retreat.

Don't go back.
Don't ever go back.
If you cross back over,
you're forever the wetback crow eater
nobody wants to stand next to,
nobody wants to know.

1 Hot Run

The passionflower diets on broken glass.

R. Jones

Teaching Composition

today my student recited choices
for restrictive clauses and nonrestrictive
clauses and somewhere around her
explanation about commas,
I remembered the first time
I saw you completely naked.
You rushed from bed to shower
before Wayne returned to catch
our clumsy ballet.
The dark pinkness
of your scrotum
I remember next,
the curious inconvenience
of that squat bundle with
its pinch of skin neatly
scoring the thing in two,
halves perfectly balanced
behind your contented penis
ridiculous with a different
kind of relief that I recognized today
in my student's eyes
when I said she was correct,
not really knowing if she'd gotten
it straight, the part
where you determine
if details removed
restrict the meaning
of one's intention,
change the way you understand
what's right in front of you.

Apologies to Ethel Mae and Her Vertebrae Which I Hit With an Umbrella When I Was Six

You confiscated it
after that,
and for the rest
of the year,
I walked to school
with only a yellow slicker
for protection when it rained,
breaking your back
on every muddy crack
that my red galoshes descended on
like shiny, rubber truncheons.

On April 1st
they sent me home
from school with fever,
and I caught you dancing
unaware of my heated presence.
Out in the sloping yard,
apple blossoms showered
the grass green as pears
where you danced alone,
hands clasped over your head,
your white cotton skirt surging,
open as you pirouetted on your toes,
a twirling, white parasol of the body.

◆ *Hollis*

our dog seems hypnotized by lace
curtains that seem to float
away from the dining room window.
They drift light as steam,
whiter than that and undulate
like a half-dressed woman
with a secret.

Hey Hollis! Wake up!
Look. Spring springs,
whenever everything merely adequate,
even you and me maybe,
might be mistaken for the amoral,
the arresting, the affluent.
Why not?

Forget winter.
forget cleaning up,
forget scrubbing down.
Run with me, now,
through the house, the yard,
the neighbor's yard too,
the neighbor who hates our dog.
It is Kerouac's spring and we need
to decompress our lungs,
feel them rise like the curtains
at the window, like kites
hell-bent for the wake
Icarus traced in his heroic meltdown.
I don't know about you , Hollis,
but I need to fly with any bird
that will have me,
surging and falling
like a swelled sail,
dirigible me
and my dirigible heart,
trusting the air.

Fishing Alone

No reel.
Nothing fancy as that.
Just an old carpet pole
cut short enough
and some fish line I unraveled
from an old spool in the shed.
I never bait the hook.
I just sit here under the willows
and watch their green tendrils
tickle the water like a woman's hair
when she's held out over deep water.
What few fish I can see
move slow enough to hammer
to death if I had a mallet.
See how they drift to the surface
as if light is what they seek,
as if I, sitting on this rock,
were as common as a stump
or old tire the river abandoned
to the gray sand and green moss?
When the sun goes down over the tops
of those pines crowding the blackberries out
along the opposite banks,
I'll be going straight home.
When he sees I caught nothing,
as usual, and he lifts his bottle
to toast my worthlessness,
this might be day his liquor
slows him down
just enough.

Son Remembers

I let him beat me
until I was too old not to hit back.
Better than pleasure I took in my own bed,
was the hot run my blood took
the first time I floored him,
this bear who could
ruin a jaw with one swipe
from his massive hands.
He hit the plank floor so hard
the good dishes rattled in the sideboard
like they did during the last mine explosion.
My mother pushed me out the door,
crammed biscuits she'd been holding,
into my open shirt and told me
to stay away at least a week,
at least until she could convince him
he'd dreamed it while drinking,
or that he'd tripped over his black boots
she'd polished that morning.
I knew the beating she'd take for that lie
would color her face for days,
but she pushed me hard as she would the mule
and said "*NOW,*" her voice low with fear.
I took off straight towards a cave
I knew he'd never find and stayed there
six days living off those
stale biscuits and blackberries.
I killed one trout and ate it raw and cold
afraid smoke would bring down the wrath
of the crazy man who cried like a baby
when I walked in the door.
He never touched me again
until he grabbed my arm
the night a stroke felled him,
killed him sure as the bullet
between his eyes I never had
quite enough hate to shoot.

Before She Was Born

Chesneys were bad news,
all the boys, bad,
the girls, foxes.
Mornings,
beer bottles collected like good
intentions around the outside stoop,
cigarette butts squashed like the tips
of stubby fingers kissed with Revlon Red.
Bladders of condoms,
festive as discarded balloons,
thubbed up against the fence where
someone tied two together with shoe string
then walked to his two-story walk-up
carrying his boots, socks white as diapers,
flashing   flashing
like rabbit tails into shadows.

Then *she* came along,
the infant of second-chance,
a silk purse out of a sow's belly.
They started to listen to concerts
on the radio and to tuck
their shirts in even on weekends,
to polish shoes together,
a conspiratorial decency
they perpetrated on each other
with a single-minded weariness
they rested from every Saturday night,

good intentions collecting on Sundays
like beer bottles around the outside stoop.

◆ *Her Brothers Who Stayed Behind*

You give up what doesn't need you.
Desire has nothing to do with it,
the taste of family
like iron on bloodied lips,
their names you keep
trying not to remember.

One Grandfather

If he is a baker
his hands will always be dusted
white as gypsum, sugar tramped
in the ridges of his soft-soled shoes.
He takes them off outside the door
before entering the upstairs apartment,
keeps his business off the carpet
as much as he is able,
leaves his shoes to the cat
who will lick them clean
as rubber spatulas,
pliant as tongues.

An Aunt Whose Name Escapes Her

Like other isolated simplicities,
she's pretty sure it's one syllable,
like the cry she made when
Aunt What? slapped her face
rosy from heat rising in the concrete
courtyard behind the bakery
where she visited some afternoons.
All she did was ask *whose violin*
when she discovered it,
a woman's curved, stringed
torso in a closeted trunk,
the one Aunt Why? locked like a diary,
warned her away from,
warned her to forget about
as completely, as obviously
as she had her manners,
those lapses in rudeness
she would take out and wear
like white gloves to a matinee
later at the Albee Theatre on Fountain Square.

She saw "The Ten Commandments,"
fell in love with Charlton Heston,
memorized the way he raised
his hands and the Red Sea parted,
shadows of rushing waters passing
over his face like clouds.

◆ *At the Other Grandfather's Door*

If you talked to Gustav
about anything and it was Saturday,
he would tell you he didn't give a shit
about religions, about politics
as long as you weren't a damn commie,
that he didn't give a rat's ass
if you were an honest man or not,
but he *would* ask what kind of beer
you drank, did you feed it to the kids
to watch them spin like new pennies
across the kitchen linoleum,
weren't they funny as hell?
Then, *Are you sober?* and if you nodded
he'd offer you a quart bottle of cold lager,
hand you what fueled him through
his hazy days—that and sausage,
black bread, and a prayer
for all the dead cousins war ate
like a wolf hiding in woods just outside
his brass-bolted door.
Four beers later he'd howl for you
and ask if the sound seemed familiar,
then follow you home, a sly shadow
just at the corner of your eye.

◆ *The Curse*

Morning unwraps you
from the mummy cloths
you sleep in all night.
After the shower,
the shave, the polish
you give to your teeth
as if they were holy relics
to be displayed to sycophants,
you robe the pink peaches
of your balls in cotton briefs,
your limbs in a worsted suit
and set off like Boris Karloff
to scare up a living
out there in the catacombs
we call the world.

When you stagger back
through the portal
after light deserts you,
the kiss you dust on my cheek
wakes me up and all the spells
break like two-thousand year
old amphorae.

Ben

six foot one,
straight as a pine,
fickle as a young horse,
tomorrow you will drive to school
one more unremarkable day.
You will come home
ravenous as a Hun.
Supper is the booty,
the spoils of the day I surrender
to the bottomless pit you are.
When despite warnings not to,
you brush your hair over my sink,
I'll sweep the fine, blonde threads up
into a tissue which I'll add to the others
folded like tiny, white flags
along the bottom drawer of my bureau,
next to the red baby-sneakers size zero,
an impossible number for a newborn
whose feet were as long as his shin.

Every afternoon I watch the road,
but I never see you coming.

Before the Knife

that morning
when steel and rubber
machination
ceased flooding your arteries
and your newly
jump-started heart
pumped like a wily,
sanguine tug on its own
as it pulled you back to us
through dark waters
of which you say
you have no memory,
before you were retooled,
the surgical nurse asked *me*
to swab the white canvas
of your small chest,
to paint with orange antiseptic
exactly where the surgeon
would work his bloody arts.

Propelled by faith,
by circumstance,
by inevitability,
I became Abraham
leading Isaac to that flat stone.
As they walked he grasped his son's trusting hand
as they talked about the unexpectedly perfect weather,
how beautiful the rising disc of sun glowed
as it burned fiercely over the distant hills.

Favoring Andy, Husband No. 2

isn't easy because he's dead
and it's hard to buy socks for somebody
marching to eternity in paper wing-tips.
Buying socks, Edith said, shows love.
It's the inconsequential things that tell a man
you think about him, all about him, all of him,
even his callused, long-nailed bunioned feet
smelly from work boots too long in standing water,
too long without a polish or, at least, foot powder.
Favoring even the worst parts of somebody who lets himself
go like that is sure to pave your way to heaven with rose
petals soft enough to ensure that when that time comes,
you'll meet up again with Andy and his paper shuffle.
Tickled by blossoms you'll stroll alongside,
barefoot as a duck.

2 First Ride

Family is the damnedest mess you'll ever have to clean up after.

Ethel Mae Smith Scherz Kennedy

◆ *May*

like a pretty girl
who's skipped out
without paying her rent
leaves us her green skirts,
lush and full
sashaying in breezes
balmy as a one-night stand
we remember whenever
a stray strand of perfume
floats in to us like music
from a neighbor's radio
when we sneak over to pick
a handful of their gardenias
which litter the grass
like white anklets tossed
carelessly to a carpeted floor.

Hitting the Deck

slow as a young cat
with nothing to chase,
the young girl next door stretches
out on her sundeck.
She elongates,
long and limber
as an open mouth
with little to say.
Then, like her modesty,
she slips off her t-shirt
to brown the white cones
of her wintery breasts,
small and specific as fists.

Sissy

pretends that we were born in another time,
that all the rules we follow
are meant to protect
civilization
the way a cotton
runner does a fine
mahogany table
around which
we all sit
sharpening
our wits
and our
knives.

Vanities

And in the lake many pearls are found
which men place in their ears.
Nennius

We have not come to shop
but to offer up
to the Piercing Pagoda
two perfect ears:
deflower with pin and cork
plump, naked lobes.

As the pin takes flesh,
Kate's pinched eyes open.
The pin wounds again.
Before the pearl stud
is screwed in place,
one perfect comma,
silk red
wells up.

She climbs down,
enters with shining eyes
a life pearlescent,
a world of gold hoops and diamond drops
that she will wear in pairs,
that she will wear with her hair tied back.

Her Mother's Lament

Effie's always been prettier than me.
Tall like her daddy
she walks jaunty as a kite flying
with no particular place to go,
but cocky, working up to it.
She's smart as a boy,
so I like her to stay home,
take care of the little ones.
She reads to them better than me,
but when she's not allowed to go out,
I see her slide me looks hateful
as those jailbirds on the chain gang.
With a deputy standing by,
those boys work on the roads,
and when we pass them on our way to town,
I've caught her winking back at them,
sly as a snake edging up on trapped prey.
She's my own flesh and blood,
but before God, I say she'll come to no good,
those big blue eyes, heavy-lidded and cool,
her long legs curved as front porch spindles:
and too big for her age,
her breasts, white as June clouds,
float over the edge of every blouse
she manages to leave open as our front door.
Some boy, slick as waxed tile,
is going to sweep her off those feet
and right on to her back.
Quick as a cold shower,
she'll end up like me,
feeling mostly used up,
rubbery as an old girdle
and as interesting as dirt.

First Ride

Them young girls riding around all hours
with them boys is trouble asking for trouble.
Elsie Smith, 1929

1
Nobody told me
it would be like this,
wind so fast through my hair
I feel like a hawk making for sky.
And him.
Sweeter than oil
slick and dangerous
on the tips of my fingers.
I told him we better not
smoke but we did anyway.
Every night for a week.

2
All weekend in Chattanooga.
Didn't we though?
Glad-ragged as a whore,
as pretty as one,
I feathered his cap
Friday to Monday morning.
When he took me home,
my momma sat crying.
Pops did 30 days
in Jackson for shooting
off the back most of his left heel
as he lit out faster than a dog,
but not fast enough.
No matter.
That boy always did do
his best dancing
when he wasn't even on his feet.

3

Gone as my waistline,
he sends $10 every two weeks,
tells me he'll be here when the time
comes, when it comes time.
My ribs ache from being kicked
inside and out, and my breasts,
the most beautiful things
he said he ever saw,
are the udders of a stupid cow
who spilled her milk at the first
sure touch of hands that knew
exactly where they were going.

Binges

Hiding in the woods
after Saturday night binges,
is Effie's way
of aggravating the shit
out of her old man.
He'll cut willow to whip
the orneriness out of her
and like a runaway cat
who vaguely remembers
the hand that's fed her,
she'll sneak slowly back
toward him where,
shirt off against the heat,
he stands waiting on the back porch.
He whittles on the end of the green wood,
and occasionally snaps it over his head
like a jockey about to race his prize mare,
both eyeing each other,
wary and ready.

Some Sunday mornings
she knows he's thought about
tracking her. Once she found
his bootprints, clear and deep
leading to the edge of the woods.
He just called, *Effie, Effie,*
would not go in without the dogs,
and he lost them at cards.
These are facts that like her,
sometime get away from him.

She usually sets out before dawn,
but she never goes far.
The river is too wide
to swim and by the time
she gets there,

she's sobered up enough
to remember the babies
she's left sleeping in the house.
So she sits,
feet dangling like trout
suspended in the slow water.
She watches the sky brighten
as slowly as faces heated by the long flush
whiskey bestows to those
who love it long and faithfully.
When it's daylight,
full and awesome,
she picks the moss from her hair
then starts the walk back,
humming lullabies all the way.

Effie Swears

she could love you
like a young girl,
giddy and gawky,
her smile as simple
and guileless as a nun.
She could show you
adolescent adoration
shot through with yearning
so transparent you could see
her heart as clearly as the yellow finch
scuttling leaves in the sweet gum out back.
She could peel desire from you
as awkwardly as the first time
stripping a peach of its fuzz.

But she is forty full
and well into fidelity
that rides her shoulder
like a pet monkey
chained daintily to her wrist,
so that when she shakes your hand
or reaches for your undoing,
her monkey coos into her ear,
sweeps his tail
across her spine
provoking goosebumps
as blind to age
as she could make you.

She could.

Their Fathers Were Beautiful

No children,
Ruby claims,
worth keeping.
But she's delivered four
I know of which always amazed me
in the wake of her stunning homeliness.
Their fathers were beautiful,
she admits, and I believe her because
each child could be Raphael's.
Her own charms still glow
like a votive candle
under smoked glass.
After two cups,
the red wine trips
a hidden mechanism that
turns her back twenty years
and the flush to her cheeks
becomes irresistible as peaches,
lush, ripe.
When I tell her this,
she takes my hand to her breast,
soft as excelsior,
and tells me if I were a man
oh, she would show me
a thing or two,
and I can't help but be convinced.
In the glow of her quiet burn,
I believe.

Duet

Ensel and Bernard
wait outside softly playing
the banjo and fiddle
she gave them.
Her white Pomeranian
chained to a tree
barks and barks and barks.
The day, just brightening
through the window panes,
criss-crosses the table,
a chessboard of light.
The chaise where the old woman
dies slowly has been moved to the porch.
She has asked to see the roses,
and it is easier to move her
than the bushes she forbids
anyone to cut into,
the same way she forbids
doctors to prune her disease.
What little there is left of her
burns away,
recedes as I watch.
I turn to touch her shawl
she pointed to moments before,
and when I turn back,
I see that I am alone.

The coffee cools in a green-enamel cup
your hands cradle as I tell you
she is gone, and in the yard
the dog barks   barks,
and the bluegrass music
has never stopped.

◆ Their Mother

When he leaves her,
so does her reason.
She slips into
the murky channels of madness.
Those she leaves on shore,
three children alone,
learn to swim,
to negotiate tricky currents,
to love sun warming their faces
as they float with congenial uneasiness
exactly where they see her disappear,
exactly where she parts the waves,
folds into them like a fish
that has been held out of water for love,
held out to see light prickle silver scales,
then released, changed and unchanged,
back to her element,
back to where she can breathe.

The children grow vigilant,
watch their own sleek bodies
for dark gashes,
anything resembling gills.

3 *Swimming Past God*

No one easily/ survives love

G. Kinnell

Almost Born Again

My clothes lie neatly folded like worn flags
on the front seat of an old Plymouth. With
the whole baptismal class, naked as shorn
sheep under our white robes, I wait for the
storm to hit. Two days now it's been coming
on, and today dawns gusty, threatening.
But redemption won't wait. The young preacher
wades hip-deep in muddy water that swirls
around him like the inevitable
overhead. The sinner in front of me
slips off his loafers as easily as
his Catholicism when the preacher
calls him to the shallows. Praising God and
damning papists, Rev. Cobb submerges,
keeps Clifford under deepening eddies,
calls on Jesus to raise this poor, mortal
wretch to the clear summit of his mighty
kingdom. He baptizes Clifford in the
name of ghosts and eleven disciples,
one by one. A pale hand bursts from under
the water. The man of god warns devils
away from those re-born, invites the pure
of heart to witness the miracle of
faith redeemed. A second hand emerges
from the river and waves wildly to God.

Rev. Cobb prays on as the wind picks up.
A dead catfish, cut line looping from his
mouth a yard from my feet, glistens like a
well-polished gun barrel. The wind rushing
through the pines at our back, whistles as though
a train behind schedule. Clifford's robe
suddenly boils up, a snow-white pennant
semaphoring to the rest of us. The
current hoists it along downstream. With both
hands raised, dripping, the preacher begs heaven
to take in, when it's time, Clifford, whose face,

surfacing, floats away, a wide-eyed moon
that sails right on past the deacon in red
suspenders who picks the wrong time to sneeze.

It takes five minutes to get to Clifford
downriver, clinging to a willow stump
and mad as hell. As we gather again
at the river, lightning strikes a live oak
across the water. The congregation,
except for Rev. Cobb and me, runs for
cover. Rev. Cobb stands his ground, shouts my
name. I lock eyes with the fish. Neither blinks,
but I get the message. Cut bait. Run. *Run.*

In the Eye of a Winter Storm

Snow defeats travel.
Watch how the tinned wings
plane glide on ice up.
See how the hotels become home,
all those televisions
warming up like so many hearths
where passengers cool their heels,
wait for room service to fire up,
to leave covered steak and fruit
outside their suite doors
like so many catered desires
caught in the eye of a winter storm
which postpones arrival,
destination a stamped declaration
their tickets remind them waits
like a faithful wife in her own bed,
warm fingers plumbing her own
weather-proof self,
serving up what everybody needs
regardless of what rages
right outside the window.

I Am Sure of This

If I were to live in Minneapolis
I would have to relearn the calculus of snow,

reinvent my stride when snow numbs
the earth and falls so thick no matter

where I stand I do not see my own feet.
No, if I woke up and discovered St. Paul

glistened across the river like a frosted New Jerusalem,
I would need to recast all my prayers,

say them silently, breathlessly or I would
have to watch them disappear into air so frigid

each fervent wish, or hymn of praise
would fall back on me like the loose ice chips words

must transform into when the sky freezes blue as sailfish hanging
on the walls of restaurants up and down my Carolina coast.

Almost

For one snow dipped moment
Minnesota almost feels real.
Cold, insistent as a hand in your pants,
creates the urge to snuggle against
anything at least as warm as yourself.
The city high-rises,
concrete and steel stalagmites,
stoic architectural summits
ice traffics with intimately.
Somewhere up there
an open window escapes notice,
frost deliquesces across the sill
where an old woman plays child,
licks the glass to feel her tongue stick
like raw meat. When her son,
the failed writer, finds her beyond heat,
he finally will find the story
he has searched for years to find,
his writer's block as shattered as concrete rinds,
as frozen monoliths the river carries to ice-breakers,
those crafty ships with prows
sharp and steady as winter,
just as useless when the season
breaks wide open into spring.

For a Flower Girl Posing

In the corner where she takes
cake to smear on the dress
they keep telling her
not to get soiled,
she scuffs the toes of her
sky-blue slippers against
the fellowship hall's smooth
linoleum the church waxed
for this occasion.
After the drinking begins
plump, old men pay her quarters
to dance and twirl so that her skirt
swirls up and her crinolines show.
One of the ushers slips her
champagne, which she drinks
like Kool-aid, and why shouldn't she?
He promises hopscotch
in the courtyard but
they never make it out
of the coat-closet,
where with a flashlight
he shows her honeymoon things
as if she were his little bride,
and when he leads her back to
the dancing and the laughing,
she catches the bouquet
the beautiful bride
seems to toss right to her.
The photographers love it
and they love her as she poses
with the pretty pink carnations,
delicate rose buds bound
together with white satin ribbon.
She smiles and twirls and laughs
as the flashbulbs dazzle her blind.

Gustav the Hun

There are no flowers on the star,
Only the new branches bloom.
S. Hazo

1 On Sandheger

In this respectable home
at eleven every night
your grandfather, Gustav, smokes
one, last cigarette.
He sits on the vanity stool
by the toilet.
You are twelve and wake up
for a glass of water.
He growls words too thick,
too German to understand
but leaves the room offering you
privacy, that rosetta stone
which unlocks secrets of adolescents' hearts.

On July 4th, you sleep in the guest room
your own double bed full of cousins.
Through the partly open door
you watch Gustav flick his final ash
to the porcelain bowl.
He takes one, long drag
and with the grace of art,
flicks the stubby butt into water
with one hand while the other
retrieves from billowing boxer shorts
his own, dear self and takes careful aim,
douses the Lucky Strike.
Water rushes and you see his face
redden as he stands up.
Fists swing in arcs at his side
as he goose-steps across the humid room
puzzling you when he mutters,
'Blitzkreig, Juden, blitzkreig.'

Fireworks intermittently light
up your room like heat lightning.
Through the summer screens
white smoke drifts in,
settles on your pillow and hair
yellow as the star of David
already secretly forming
on the sleeve of your heart.

2 On McMicken

Gustav, you are German down to your ich liebe dich,
so easy to say, difficult to believe.
Blue-eyed, flinty as any roof
you spend your life laying down
with tar and pitch.
You have a quick smile,
and you like what you like.
Never have I seen you eat bread
not cut from a round of rye
black as the lager you drink every weekend.
By Sunday night things go one of two ways.

We may end up at Uncle Albert's.
There, we dance to accordion
he plays bombastically
with the arrogance of a man making love
to his girlfriend in front of family.
We eat knockwurst and struedel
whose recipe is a state secret
Magdaline will not share with American in-laws.
Beer comes warm in purple crocks, which your wife,
Tennessee Ethel, Angel of the Malt and Foam,
carries up from the cellar you hide guns in.
You sing to us in German
only Albert and Magda understand.
You laugh with the abandon of a minority
afraid to show too much pleasure in public,
wise policy because this is America, 1944
where Germans are not interred like Japs,

but tolerated on city streets like spit or dogs.
This is the daily traffic of loathing and fear
you pass through, a Messershmit
flying reconnaissance over hostile territory.
You laugh all the way home and sleep
all night, snoring like the maiden aunts.
But we do not always end up at Albert's
counting beer bottles for the two cents
a piece they bring us.
The flip side of the weekend coin glitters
like that glass eye we don't want to look at.

If the beer runs out too early, or business is bad,
Sunday night is a sharp pain which pricks us
like a pin stuck in our collar.
On God's day, hatred, florid as face in stroke,
blooms over the house like bougainvillea.
Punches land with the accuracy of a drunk
focused on the only thing he can find
readily available: wives, daughters, their babies.
After fists fall, chairs or toasters fly
at heads and legs.
It becomes apparent to veterans of these small wars
that the best plan is one of strategic retreat
to the second story porch where vertigo keeps
our monster at bay.
Blankets stored under the swing
cover limbs numb with cold and kicks.
Pillows cradle dreams worn out by the time
we are twelve or fourteen like outgrown bicycles
that used to carry us everywhere we needed to go.
In winter, we learn to wear shoes in the house
all the time because evacuation is a casual thing
with short, violent notice. The neighbors keep changes
of clothing for each of us, like we do for them.
Practicality becomes the art of survivors
in times of war and this is war,
make no mistake.

In church the Pledge of Allegiance
precedes the Doxology and then our prayer
for victory for the Allies, our boys,
for 'peace in our time.'
We recite it like members
of a family whose father is blind,
and so they learn Braille
so he'll have somebody
to write to if he ever goes away.
We all pray for that miracle
like good Christians
every day, our heads bent,
hearts hardening
like day-old bread
we will taste
for the rest of our lives.

3 On Riddle Road

In Clifton, Jews were welcome as taxes
in my grandfather's house, the word Jew
ground out between teeth like sand
blown to your mouth at the beach,
or glass from a goblet you break
against your lip when you're too drunk
to remember where your mouth is.
Jew, this word I grew up believing
meant obligation you pay up for like sales
tax, the greater your total guilt,
the more penance you owed.
Our German enclave in Cincinnati
owed plenty, mortgaged to the hilt,
so books, books and more books,
glossy magazines and posters
with photos of bones blossoming
in gardens, with names like scythes,
Auschwitz, Buchenwald, Treblinka,
or Dachau spread out on blonde coffee tables;
books spread open like vestments

penitents kiss the hems of, to publicly exhibit
contrition for their crimes, like serial killers
who reveal victims' locations
in public performances of remorse.

Public I came to know as lying to strangers,
and private a place we behave the way
we really are, where,
like one pederastic priest forgiving
another in a confessional,
language becomes unholy.
Jew, that word my grandfather choked on
in conversation with his brothers, Albert and Eugene,
who privately warned me of the global conspiracy of Jews,
the liberal media stinking with them,
the money lenders, the salacious Jewboys, kikes,

pink-cheeked Albert and sweet, old Eugene
whispered not to tell my mother what they told me,
but informing me, over and over with their hatred
to what enormity man's hopelessness can grow
when it feeds on the deaths
of our small humanities to one another,
or our acquiescence to the goose-step of silence
forever storming the borders of our souls.

Albert and Gus railing against
the emergence of nation-Israel from one word, Jew,
the country I inhabit now like my own mouth,
the word I have become to settle old debts.
I cast my days like coins to the heavens and pray
for forgiveness to flower like light
from the body of stars above me.
That my new God will answer with mercy,
not justice.

Gustav's Ammo

Sit on my lap, here, he directed me
and I would sit down up on his knees.
He threw bread to the squirrels,
nickels to the young Albanese boys who crowded
around our porch like a pack of terriers
starving for everything. He told us
stories the war denied him about cousins,
brothers, of their wives, children, successes,
all fictional, all lies, all of them dead as charity
by the end of the war, the one from which he
escaped to grow fat in America.
He shingled and tarred roofs, tin
flashing neatly pinned to eaves and overhangs
bright as medals on the breasts of houses,
as nickels tossed to the boys,
as bullets Gustav carried in his pocket like change.

Her Grandfather's Afraid He's Swimming Past God

He unravels near the end
of the journey that defines him.
See him dive into the clear pool,
the silver blink of fish
weaving through shafts of sun
piercing the water like gold staves.
Like his incautious dive
to the sea when he sank
like the stones he tied
to his ankles with strong hemp
braided like his shank of hair,
light fades near the bottom
where he cut the granite ballast
from his legs and sliced free
the carrageen which promises
immortality if he eats
its bitter stalks and roots.

Soon, he will build a fire
to warm this last night
before home and then,
cook and eat his salty catch.
But now, the pool
soothes his tired
muscles weary of the road
and as he breaks the surface,
he sees his soiled clothes
clotted on the shore and a dark
quick slither retreating to brush.
He shivers as if a cloud
has passed over the sun,
but the day is bright
and eternity stretches
before him like the strong
sure strokes of his own good arms.

Stroke

It enveloped him slowly,
first a weak jaw,
then his arm limp as a dry hose,
hung loose from the shoulder.
By the time he made it in the front door
from Heinlein's package store, his foot,
locked in the concrete of his shoe,
rooted in the floor suddenly under his face
like a stone mattress chilling him.
The Life Squad dug him up,
logged him in at Christ's Hospital,
where they propped him in a corner
like a fencepost with no fence.
Later, they wheeled him to a bed
he would burn in for years,
loud and violent, language lost to him,
only the roar of rotting trunks plunging
to earth left to him and anyone present
who might listen to the savage loosed
from one side of his ravaged mind,
the one he kept trying to rebuild plank by plank,
each falling to ruin he recognized as his
body blossoming into final decay,
gardenias emerging from his fingers,
roses from his toes,
chrysanthemums his navel,
orchids from his penis,
violets at his lips, and tiny bells
of edelweiss ringed his brow like a crown
he became fond of and fingered
with his good hand each night
before falling into fragrant sleep,
his breath at the end sweet as lilac.

The Little Sisters of the Poor

Walking to the bus on Clifton we pass
by quickly, afraid of the black barge of
skirts that sweeps us up against the banks of
curbs when a great flotilla of nuns floats
down stone steps of the old Little Sisters
of the Poor. They scare us worse than priests, these
sisters married to Christ, related by
name to the poor bums who squat at the bus
stop. Like the sounds of knuckles popping these
men click their tongues at us as we all dart
by, a small school of Protestant fish who
swim away in the fearful current of
our Lutheran prejudices. We make
for the tank of our bus where, like some fluke
of aquarium carp, we press open
mouths against the window glass, working *our*
tongues back and forth like seagrass at the nuns'
brothers lined up along the walk like gulls
waiting to dive into the clear welcome
to catastrophe our mindless taunting
provokes. We're bait swimming in the tide pools.
If we press our ears against the moist glass,
we can hear the sea rushing through our hearts.

4 The Accident

This was the habitation, this is the site:
here the fat grains of maize grew high
to fall again like red hail.

P. Neruda, *The Heights of Macchu Picchu*

Elmer and Lucy

Named after a father
his southern cousins called
the "Union gimp.'

this Elmer grows tall on two legs,
loves church and a girl
he calls Lucy though her name is Mae.

He hates spring, he says,
makes him think of all that work
the farm demands like an impious woman.

He loves the yellow eddies in her hair,
which he sinks into when she lets
him brush tangles away.

She joins his church,
buys a plot in his cemetery
with his people and her father cries

when she rides her bay stallion
the morning of her wedding.
It is for that horse

that Elmer wants her,
to see a woman that beautiful
riding a horse as fast as that one,

to think they will both sleep
under roofs of his making,
will wait to turn to him

when he reaches out his hand.
in the mornings when the green trees
murmur like a hushed congregation.

One hundred years later in an old bible
a great granddaughter finds his handwriting
strong and blue in the back inside leaf,

I would stick stars on your elbows and feet,
watch you dance through the night clouds,
a redeemed Salome moving her hips not for death, but for me.

◆ *Lucy*

It is Lucy who imprints
upon her children a love of trees,
grass, sky and deer,
summer and fall,
the wintry agility
cold demands,
all things nature provides
with assiduous prudence.
They love her singing,
her bright skirts and aprons,
the soft pocket of her arms
they slip into at day's end,
her consummate motherliness
and a deeper possession,

her love of the night sky,
the way she watches stars
as if any minute she might
take off to find her own.
She allows Milly to sit
with her after the others sleep,
teaches her about Andromeda,
Cassiopeia, Big and Little Bears,
to wish on the tails of nomad
stars as they burn earthward,
to whisper those wishes
to the voiceless stones,
listening, listening.

August, 1910

Toward summer's end when the heat shimmers
like a living membrane stretched over the fields,
the house, the road, chores need to be tended to,
animals slaughtered for market, vegetables and fruit
blanched, frozen, canned. Big suppers start
every morning in the kitchen big as the small factory it
becomes when women need to cook for thirty hired-hands.

It is Milly's first summer she's allowed to help,
tall enough to reach the back burners to stir
kettles big as chamber pots, her thick hair twisted
down her back like brown hemp tied with dotted ribbon.
It's a privilege not to watch after the others.
Esmond, closest, but slow-witted, teases
her like the pet pig he raises and sells at fair.

Leila's the baby, pink as Esmond's pig,
eyes like blue buttons from the button jar,
hair like silk spiders weave in the barn.
Leila's quiet as a cat and purrs when their
mother nurses her on time on the back porch.
But Milly can't help but love Virgil best:
the blonde sweetheart for whom

she will search the rest of her life.
He sings to her when she bathes him,
never tricks the dogs, or terrorizes the hens.
His soft smile imparts the serenity of painted cherubs
staining the church windows, and he shows signs already
of a compatible reasonableness Milly loves.
He is her quiet time, the child she reads to,

who runs to greet her after school
as if she'd been gone for years.
This is what she will remember,
and the way he loves wading in the creek,
comes running through the lacy ripples,
reckless, an imperfect naturalist certain of terrain,
as if for the rest of his life he would count
on such shallow waters.

The Accident

Biscuits white as vidalias sliced
open wait on the sideboard.
Five women serve the hungry men
huddled around the table,
long boards held up with barrels draped
by white, ironed sheets.
Gallon jars of lemonade and warm beer
alternate down its bumpy length.
It's Friday and the only big supper of the week,
the rest, midday feasts of Rabelaisian proportion.

In the kitchen Milly stirs with a twelve inch
ladle the jelly boiling like oil in tarpits,
bubbles rising slowly, long
contented burps which erupt
as perfect circles in the delicious
red muck strawberries cook down to.
At the kitchen table, Virgil,
stripped to shorts for the heat,
colors inside the outlines
which Milly's drawn for him of the stars.

Hercules, Orion, Big Bear,
orange, blue and green smeared around
Virgil's mouth where he chews
color sticks down to wet, chalky stubs.
Lucy calls from the yard for Milly
to bring the rolls which she gathers,
doughy muffins in linen-lined baskets
she takes outside to the hungry help.
Out of chalk, Virgil decides

to help.
He climbs up on a chair
carefully wraps a towel around the
steel spoon as he's seen his sister do.
Standing on tip-toes he eases

the ladle into the jelly he loves,
a sweet reminder of morning.
He begins to stir, surprised
because it's harder than he thought,
the thick goo resistant, sticky.
With two hands clutching the towel

he pulls harder and harder until
his balance, like the tilting chair,
gives in to gravity.
Virgil sways away from the stove,
and if only he does not fear
falling so much, he might not
automatically grab at the kettle
as if that would stay his catastrophe
instead of ensuring it.
His steady tug and weight

on the ladle, now a lever,
a fulcrum of disaster,
leans toward the floor where
Virgil tumbles, pulling the pot
ladle and boiling preserves after him,
all over him in a slow flux which baptizes
him from the shoulders down,
sticky jelly flowing down his small trunk
like lava engulfing a sapling growing in its path.
Virgil tries to roll away, pushes the pot

from his hip with a hand he doesn't recognize
as his, glazed in red, luminous,
a delicious smell to him even as he begins
to scream more loudly than he ever heard
Esmond scream when he fell from the tree,
a scream that stops, then begins again,
louder and more high-pitched,
a sound that reminds Milly

of rabbits when the dog hunts
them down for sport,

a sound she will echo
when she runs to the kitchen
and sees Virgil, knees to chest
screaming and screaming,
beautiful in his rosy agony,
the small curve of his body
a defiant fire-bowl one field hand
will douse with beer, then lemonade from the table
anything to wash the jelly off,
anything to stop the screaming child,

the wailing women, the suddenly silent girl striking
the table with a ladle like a drum she means
to play until she beats it into the ground.

Blame

There is never a moment's
hesitation in calling it
no one's fault.

Lucy called Milly out,
Milly is only a child herself,
Virgil knows better than to
play around the stove.

They will assign blame
later when Virgil has been
cleaned up and calmed down.

Burns are common accidents
and this one seems no worse
than the one Turley's daughter, Jane,
suffered last spring when her dress

caught a cinder from stumps
burning in a field and they had to
dress her wounds through July.

Only her arms and neck scarred.
Collars and sleeves will hide that,
her father's rich farmland
and lush orchards dowry

enough to compensate
a boy more true
than the one who moved on.

What Milly remembers
after Jane visits and shows
Lucy her ruined arms,
is what her mother says

after Jane leaves,
something about lucky but marred,
about how all the apples in the world
cannot make her beautiful.

Elmer

Elmer is the one who lifts
Virgil from the sink
where they have been
drowning him in cool water,
trying to tell where to swab
jelly away and where not to,
where the skin peels away
translucent as steamed onion.

He carries his son to the horse trough
and immerses him to his neck,
all the while batting the women
away with their good intentions
and ineffectiveness.
What amazes Elmer is the noise,
how one small child can create
such deviant howls,

lupine and constant.
As he cups water around Virgil's
lips urging him to drink, to quiet,
he remembers a young horse
he had as a boy,
how it wandered off tract,
got trapped in a wolf snare,
how he too howled in fear, pain,

his eyes, like Virgil, accusatory,
wild and attenuated to the swooping
brutality overwhelming them,
a look impossible but irrefutable
in the face of his four year old son,
a glaze of hatred and desire for relief,
a passion of such ferocious blasphemy
that later Elmer will convince himself

he imagined it, imagined it all away
as if none of this were happening,
as if it were happening again and again.

◆ *Milly*

Daddy's left him to me for now.
Torn strips of old sheets
to dip in spring-house water,

the coolest we've got,
the only thing that keeps
his screams low,

more like a whimper
the dog made after a neighbor's buggy
nipped him at the hip.

Virgil's naked on the divan,
the softest thing we could think of.
Mom's got him slathered up with butter,

made me do it after she touched him
and skin came away with the gauze.
He's pink as crawdad boiled alive.

He's pink from the neck down,
and when he pees himself,
he screams like somebody's

sprayed iodine on him.
He won't drink anything.
He just lies there,

arms away from his body
as if even the thought of his own
arm against his side would hurt.

I want to go outside,
run down to the creek
and bring back a bucket

of the icy waters.
But Dad says I'm to stay put,
that the only thing which calms

him down is me sitting here
where he can see me,
where I can smell the butter,

thick and creamy sweet
glossing him all over
so he looks unreal,

a kewpie doll with cloudy stars
where there should be eyes.

The Second Day

The morphine lessens the noise
impossibly constant and shrill.
Sleep is a dream Milly imagines as she
sits near Virgil's perfect face,
at turns, singing, praying, pleading.
The couch is soaked where she has poured
the cool waters over his arms and legs,
his chest, only the groin spared.
Lucy disappears to feed Leila.
Esmond sneaks occasionally in to stare
as if the scene were a play
he was memorizing for school.
At lunch he brings Milly a roll sliced
and stuffed with thick cheese and ham.
When she rises to take it,
Virgil moans louder so she sits
again to eat, suddenly ravenous,
indifferent to the sour smells around her,
drinks long draughts from a mug Elmer
refills periodically when he rises from his chair.
He's been told what to expect and this failure
to help his own son paralyzes him,
sends him to the Bible for explanation he can't find.

Lucy's taken to the bedroom with the babies,
uses the backstairs to avoid the parlor,
seems distracted as if they have company
she's careful not to disturb.
And Milly, his poor Milly.
He will lift her soon if need be,
to take her to bed,
dose her with the laudanum Doc Higgins
left and take her place next to Virgil.
Beyond this, he sees little.
It takes him five minutes before he
feels Milly's head on his knee,
arms gripping his calf as if she were falling,
a ravine opening up in front of them

like a sinkhole under a trail they trust,
that they used to find their way home on
in the dark and it occurs to him
that there is no whiskey in the house,
that's been a long time
since he's been really drunk,
that he's never been drunk in a cemetery.

The Second Night and Third Day

Milly sleeps on the floor next to Virgil.
A slop jar near her head doesn't seem to matter.

Virgil still rocks, but drugged, quieter
than he's been since the accident.

Elmer sits in the kitchen when Lucy
descends the back stairs for water.

They don't say anything to each other,
just look past the other's ear as if direct
contact would flay their eyes.

Lucy pumps a pitcher of water as if
she were trying to rip it out of the floor.

Elmer sinks further into himself,
lowers his head to his folded arms

like a small child told to put
his head down at school.

Neither speaks. Neither makes any more
sound than they need to as Lucy
passes by on her way back upstairs.

She wants to touch him,
wants to lay her hands on his neck,

and he would hold her if he could,
but some alien ghost of tragedy

takes up residence in their world
where suddenly unsavory shadows

beckon just at the corner of their eyes,
spontaneous fortresses where hours before
open fields hosted blue bells and queen's lace.

By morning, Virgil struggles to breathe.
The doctor says his lungs have filled up,

that his fever will not break,
that the sounds he makes now

tell how little more he will suffer,
tell them to start making the plans

no one really believes yet are necessary.
The doctor sees he is talking to people
exhausted and grieving, insensible as rock.

As he leaves the father asks when,
and he answers soon but he knows

it cannot be soon enough,
that time is an enemy or voices
some imagine assaulting heaven.

Afternoon

The sun moves slowly toward the black walnuts
Lucy has wanted to take down since she first saw
that they blocked sunsets from this front room window.
Elmer argued they shaded the cows so she let it go,
would ride out past the leggy copse to watch

light sink inevitably beyond touch,
like Virgil sinking now, breath slower and slower,
a gurgle rising from his chest like a small
spring pushing through clay at its source.
She worries about Milly lying beside him

whispering to him, telling him stories,
smoothing his blonde hair slick from sweat,
and the water Milly keeps trickling over his body,
careful not to touch the skin darkening, crusty
with healing which ridiculously, already has begun.

Milly hasn't slept for more than an hour
at a time since the accident and appears to Lucy
like one of the young widows she sees in church,
beautiful, but hopelessly diminished.
She wishes Elmer would stop neighbors coming in

with food and condolence because the house
looks like the house of the dead,
a wake in progress, or memorial feast.
Kitchen noises and hushed voices filter in
like the fading light, and Lucy realizes

suddenly that Milly's soft cadence has stilled,
that the room is absolutely silent,
that the silence is so complete her own breath
comes echoing back to her as loud and booming
as Elmer banging on a washtub to call the children

to supper or to see the new cow give birth.
He wanted them to see it,
hear the rangy bawl the calf assaulted

their ears with, and Lucy almost can hear it,
then does hear it and can't tell

when it began, only that it comes from some
place inside her so dark she can't see it,
the only thing visible at this moment her oldest
child cradling her dead one and keening,
rocking as if to settle him into sleep.

◆ *Under the Sweet Gum*

Elmer allows no one but himself
to dig this hole under the sweet
gum he planted for Virgil.
For each child, a tree:
Milly, a willow,
Esmond, oak,

Virgil, sweet gum
and Leila, a white birch by
Fat Goose Creek.
Denouncing heaven,
he will not surrender Virgil to the church yard,
doesn't want a preacher,

but Lucy won't come without one.
The ladies' circle has tried to soften
the black dirt vulgar in its raw nakedness.
White sheets billow against
the sides of the grave, dozens of nosegays
bound with white satin ribbons

pinned to the sheet so that walls which define the grave
seem more like an arbor or enclosed garden,
a shady resting place where
sun changes the color of grass
as it moves through the day.
It will be these nosegays Milly

watches as they lower Virgil slowly,
ropes unhitching easily
as the pine box settles in.
It will be the sight, the smell of corsages,
daylilies or gladiolus that will sicken
Milly for the rest of her life.

She will refuse them at her own wedding,
never wear them in her hair or at her breast,
but right now she thinks how beautiful they are,
how Virgil loves bright colors,
how he will want to draw them
when he gets back home.

◆ *Mildred*

How she mourns her brother
from the black chasm she falls into,
how when she tries to climb out
her hands will grab small bouquets
which detach so that she lurches backwards,
tumbles down to the pine horror where

Virgil knocks twice, then three times,
as he used to on her door at night
when she would take him out to the old well
and show him how the stars were born there,
tiny and bright as Lucy's cut-glass
earrings in their black-velvet case.

How she tries to open Virgil's casket
tries, really tries, but how impossible
to do so while she stands on it,
how she can't climb out and the flowers
keep tearing away from the sheets and into her hands.
How later she explains to her husband

why she sleeps only on white sheets,
why she returns all those wedding gifts
of perfectly wrapped, flowered sheets
to bewildered friends who learn to accept
her eccentricity but never learn
why no one calls her Milly.

The day after Virgil dies, Lucy demands
that Elmer sell the horse for whatever he can get,
that he donate the money to the First Presbyterian Church,
that he leave the house if he hates prayer circles and bible study
she will host three times a week until Elmer dies thirty-five
  years later
when she moves back to Stuart until her kidneys kill her

at sixty-eight with her own poisoned blood.
Neighbors describe Mildred as solemn,

but indelicate, agree that nursing suits her
even if she does get airs
at the State Hospital where she learns
to give shots that heal,

to listen for consumption, pneumonia
and never once, even when she marries,
even in her marriage bed where she learns
how love, a sharp and sterile knife,
can cauterize old wounds,
will ever be Milly again.

On the way back from the sweet gum,
that newly dead space under that tree,
her mother yanks her hair,
grabs her by the shoulders,
warns her she is Mildred now,
and Mildred she better stay

or she might hear that name, *Milly*,
that voice, howling *Milly, Milly,*
in the night for the rest of whatever life
God saw fit to leave her,
that it was time to put off childish
things and take up with the Lord,

who had damned her to hell
for killing her little brother,
that it was all her fault,
would always be her fault,
that God might not recognize her as Mildred,
that it was her only chance for salvation,

the only ruse left her.
Then Lucy lets her go so suddenly
Mildred falls to the grass,
falls to the sweet, damp grass
where she rests until she hears Elmer's call to supper,
the loud steel knell rolling across the fields like a storm.

◆ *In Pennsylvania Spring Comes Hard*

like a memory you work at,
fixing on a reluctant notion
or coy recollection resisting,
like tulips that give into April
slowly.
They lie there, gradually
aroused by something warm
prodding them toward the brief exhibitionism
it is their nature to exhibit.
When they flash
their particular fleshy quality,
the colors are lost on you.
All you can see is the floral come-on,
the promise primavera.

You shudder,
memory opening out.

About the Author

Linda Lee Harper received her Master of Fine Arts from the University of Pittsburgh, where she was awarded an Academy of American Poets First Prize. She has taught in the English departments of the University of Pittsburgh and the University of South Carolina at Aiken. Recently she served as editor of the poetry journal *The Devil's Millhopper.*

Winner of numerous prizes and honors, she has been published in such literary magazines as the *Georgia Review, Passages North,* and *International Quarterly.* Her first chapbook, *A Failure of Loveliness,* won the William and Kingman Page Chapbook Award from Nightshade Press. She currently lives in Knoxville, Tennessee, with her husband and two children, Katy and Ben.

About the Artist

Barbara Kerne, painter and print artist, is a Professor of Art at Montgomery College in Rockville, Maryland. Represented by Addison/Ripley Fine Art in Washington, DC, she has exhibited her work nationally and internationally. Public and private collectors of her work include the Corcoran Gallery of Art and the Library of Congress in Washington, DC; the Norton Gallery of Art in West Palm Beach, Florida; and the Portland Museum of Art in Portland, Oregon.

Toward Desire is the winner of the 1995 Word Works Washington Prize. Linda Lee Harper's manuscript was selected from 326 manuscripts submitted by American poets.

FIRST READERS:
Celia Brown
Jamie Brown
Donald Cunningham
Wayne Drozinski
Pat Gray
Steve Hester
Tod Ibrahim
Hiram Larew
Sydney March
Steven B. Rogers
Martha Sanchez-Lowery

SECOND READERS:
Jim Henley
Reuben Jackson
Elaine Magarrell

FINAL JUDGES:
Karren L. Alenier
J.H. Beall
James Hopkins – Co-Director
Miles David Moore – Co-Director
Robert Sargent
Hilary Tham

Other Books in the Word Works series

Alenier, Karren L.	*Wandering on the Outside*
* Goldberg, Barbara	*Berta Broadfoot and Pepin the Short: A Merovingian Romance*
** McEuen, James	*Snake Country*
* Magarrell, Elaine	*Blameless Lives*
* Marchant, Fred	*Tipping Point*
* Moore, Barbara	*Farewell to the Body*
** Moore, Miles David	*The Bears of Paris*
* Rogoff, Jay	*The Cutoff*
Sargent, Robert	*Aspects of a Southern Story*
Sargent, Robert	*Woman From Memphis*
* Shomer, Enid	*Stalking the Florida Panther*
** Tham, Hilary	*Bad Names for Women*
* White, Nancy	*Sun, Moon, Salt*

*Washington Prize winners
**Capital Collection

Word Works Anthologies:

Alenier, Karren L.	*Whose Woods These Are*
Bursk, Christopher	*Cool Fire* (A chapbook from the Creative Center for Non-Violence workshop)
Dor, Moshe; Leshem, Giora; Goldberg, Barbara	*The Stones Remember*
Parry, Betty	*The Unicorn and the Garden*

Requests for our brochure and other information must be accompanied by a self-addressed stamped envelope.

About the WORD WORKS

The Word Works, a nonprofit literary organization, publishes contemporary poetry in collector's editions. Since 1981, the organization has sponsored the Washington Prize, an award of $1,000 to a living American poet. Each summer, Word Works presents free poetry programs at the Joaquin Miller Cabin in Washington, DC's Rock Creek Park. Annually, two high school students debut at the Miller Cabin Series as winners of the Young Poets Competition.

Since Word Works was founded in 1974, programs have included: "In the Shadow of the Capitol," a symposium and archival project on the African-American intellectual community in segregated Washington, DC; the Gunston Arts Center Poetry Series (including Ai, Carolyn Forché, Stanley Kunitz, Linda Pastan, among others); the Poet-Editor panel discussions at the Bethesda Writer's Center (including John Hollander, Maurice English, Anthony Hecht, Josephine Jacobsen, among others); Poet's Jam, a multi-arts program series featuring poetry in performance; and many other events and educational programs such as a poetry workshop at the Center for Creative Non-Violence (CCNV) shelter.

Past grants have been awarded by the National Endowment for the Arts, the National Endowment for the Humanities, the DC Commission the Arts and Humanities, the Witter Bynner Foundation, and others, including many generous private patrons.

Word Works is a member of the Poetry Committee of the Greater Washington, DC Area which is centered at the Folger Shakespeare Library. The WORD WORKS has established an archive of artistic and administrative materials in the Washington Writing Archive housed in the George Washington University Gelman Library.

Please enclose a self-addressed, stamped envelope with all inquiries.